Millennial Warrior

By Jasmin Rosario

HeartInk Press LLC

Since 2009
Tallahassee • Plant City

Copyright © 2022 by Jasmin Rosario

All rights reserved. This book is protected under the copyright laws of the United States of America. This book may not be copied or reprinted for commercial gain or profit. No portion of this book may be reproduced, stored in a retrieval system, or transmitted in any form or by any means—electronic, mechanical, photocopy, recording, scanning, or other—without the prior written permission of the author. Brief quotations in critical reviews or articles are not permitted without the consent of the author. Permissions will be granted upon request.

EIN: 978-1-7370620-6-6

Heart.Ink Press, LLC
www.heartinkpress.com
Tuned to the beat of your heart
Manifesting dreams and visions

Printed in the United States of America

Table of Content

Kingdom Mindset

Your Kingdom Come	pg. 8
The Chosen Ones	pg. 13
Faith	pg. 19
The Key of the House of David	pg. 23
The Potter's Hand	pg. 28
Don't Become a Pillar of Salt	pg. 33
A New Mindset	pg. 36
Invite Jesus to Supper	pg. 41
Communion	pg. 45

Teach These Fingers to War

Not by Might nor by Power…The Spirit God	pg. 50
A Cup of Water	pg. 55
The Lord's Anointed	pg. 60
How the Mighty Have Fallen	pg. 67
Who Am I	pg. 71
Mighty Warrior	pg. 76
Humility	pg. 80
Marching Orders	pg. 84
Fearless Warrior	pg. 88
The Power of Worship and Praise	pg. 92

Kingdom

Mindset

Your Kingdom Come

Matthew 6:10, "Thy Kingdom come thy will be done, on earth as it is in heaven."

According to the Strong Concordance, 932, the Greek word for kingdom is basileia. Basileia is a realm and dominion. As people of the kingdom of God, we are to carry out the will of God. We accomplish this by taking dominion on this earth over our lives, families, and cities. The earth is the Lord and everything in it belongs to him. So, we are to take our authority through Jesus and advance the kingdom of God on this earth and take our rightful place as sons and daughters of God. Revelation 5:10 says, "And you have caused them to become a Kingdom of priests for our God. And they will reign on the earth." We are called to be priests who must come before God with clean hands and a pure heart. Jesus came as a worthy lamb who was slain for our sins. He is the mediator between heaven and earth, all who call on the name of Jesus are saved. We are pure because the blood of Jesus purifies us which gives us our rightful sonship. God created us in his image and likeness and when we received salvation by faith through Jesus Christ, we were given Christ's authority. Authority to cast out demons, lay hands on the sick and see them recover, and to change our region and atmosphere by opening our mouths. Jesus taught the disciples how to pray, and he taught them the Lord's prayer. Matthew 6:10 says, "Thy kingdom come thy will be done." Jesus is showing us to pray his will. In order to pray God's will over our lives and on this earth, we have to call forth for God's Kingdom to come. We are calling forth for God's realm and dominion to come into our earthly realm. We live in the world, but we are not of the world. As sons of God, we are set apart from this world. This requires salvation, concentration, and sanctification. We are renewed by God's word, and we are transformed by His Spirit. We have to submit to God's authority so that we are made whole, and in his likeness, so that we can create God's Kingdom here on earth, so that God's will is being done all over the earth especially in the church of Christ.

You cannot have dominion given over to you if you do not have a Kingdom mindset. 2 Corinthians 4:18 states, "So we fix our eyes on what is seen, but on what is unseen, since what we see is temporary, but what is unseen is eternal." The unseen are the mysteries of God, the downloads of heaven for your life, the heart of God, and the will of God. To attain these things, we have to go from glory to glory. This means we have to reach higher into the glory realms so that the mysteries of God are revealed. So that wealth, breakthrough, healing, and elevation are poured into our earthly storehouses. These are all a part of the Kingdom of God.

Submission and obedience to the Lord are very important keys in developing a kingdom mindset. Submitting means that we are yielding ourselves to a superior authority, which is God. We are allowing Him to be the authority and ruler in our lives. This is not an enslaved mindset; it just means we recognize we are dependent on the one who created us, and we were created to give him glory. God created the heavens and the earth, and all the glory goes to him. His glory and goodness are in the creation of God. That means within his goodness is his understanding, knowledge, counsel, might, and wisdom. This submission results in us honoring God for his name, glory and who he is. Because we fear the Lord, meaning we revere his superiority, we gain wisdom. Those who are wise will not follow instructions or advice from the wicked but only the counsel of the godly. Following godly counsel causes us to obey God in every aspect of our life: personal, family, financial, health, and ministry.

There are people who willfully disobey God and have unrealistic expectations for God to pull them out of trouble and bless them. He blesses his righteous children, the ones who are right standing with Him. Part of having a kingdom mindset is obedience to every instruction God gives.

Our own disobedience leads us to torments, disgrace, and curses because we are walking outside of God's will, outside of his protection. So, we are now open targets to attacks and tormenting spirits. This causes people to be connected and in covenant with places and things that we are not supposed to be connected to. Oftentimes when coming out of disobedience, having a repented heart and being forgiven, God will give an instruction. Sometimes, the instruction is not what we would prefer for ourselves. To choose to go against the will of God usually means that person wants to selfishly choose their own will. All that is doing is delaying the promises God has for his righteous servants. We must shift our perspective on submission and obedience because a kingdom mindset has a heavenly perspective. Jeremiah 29:11 tells us that "God has plans to prosper you and not to harm you." Romans 8:28 informs us that "God works all things for the good of those who love him and are called according to his purpose." In the wilderness, God does the greatest healing and transformations. This is part of his process of the anointing and preparation to receive the promises of God. Shift your perspective into a godly one and allow Him to work in you. God gives us exceedingly and abundantly more than we ask for according to our faith (Ephesians 3:20). So, we have to believe God wholeheartedly; trust him with complete faith and allow him to mold us into a whole and completely new person in

Christ in the wilderness season. God is with us, not against us, and you will not be put to shame, but in due season be exalted for His glory. Kingdom people, recognize that we are a work in progress and that we must endure in our internal spiritual process as God grows us and matures us for our next seasons, opportunities, and open doors that He has for us.

The Chosen Ones

Exodus 4:10, "And Moses said unto the Lord, "O my Lord, I am not eloquent, neither heretofore, nor since, thou hast spoken unto thy servant: But I am slow of speech, and slow of a tongue."

To do God's work for his Kingdom to come, he commissions people to help accomplish this work. God doesn't choose someone based on education, talent, or race. He picks whom he pleases to pick. He picks the ones that he knows will do his work; the ones who will not turn away no matter the temptation. There are many people who have been commissioned to do God's Kingdom work. Prophetically, we are living in a time of a great exposure being done in this world to bring forth revival, especially concerning the United States. There are people of God who have sold out to the world system. How do you recognize this? You listen to their messages and theology. Those who have an ear to hear, in other words those who have discernment can hear the watering down of the message, the perversity in the message, the hateful delivery, et cetera. In Matthew 7:15-20, Jesus warns to beware of false prophets. A prophet is someone who delivers God's word. The prophet is a part of the five-fold ministry mentioned in Ephesians 6:20, some apostles, prophets, evangelist, pastor, and teachers. In this instance, the prophet is referred to as looking out for prophets that claim to be of God, but speak false prophecy carrying a spirit of Jezebel, a spirit of witchcraft. It also can refer to anyone speaking God's word. The riches of this world have gotten many of these commissioned people of the Lord drunk with the lust of flesh and with the greed of money. They have begun to conform to the world instead of remaining transformed by the renewing of their mind.

    Jesus is coming and the way for the return of Christ needs to be paved, and the Body of Christ must be without blemish and without wrinkle according to Ephesians 5:27. God is seeking for the ones who will conform to his way and the hearts that are on fire for him. He is searching for those who have a broken past, but they are people after God's heart who didn't allow their past sins and trauma to define them. The people who rose out of the grave, into the light, and are faithful with the little God has called them to do. These people do not speak false prophecy and are not bound with wickedness or operate in manipulation known as a spirit of witchcraft. The hearts of this remnant have been made new, made into a heart of flesh that Jesus has given to them. They are so sold out for God; they boldly proclaim the gospel with a spirit of truth. These people bring up issues that the world calls controversial, that outwardly seem to divide people, but are awakening the slumbering souls. The controversial issues the world acclaims are transgenderism, homosexuality, women are free to sleep around as a statement of freedom, abortion, and pedophiles. These mighty men and women of God are unashamed and brave enough to speak out to the world that these matters are wrong, and set to destroy mankind's immorality in this nation, United States, and all over the world. These people are not cowards, they are not sowing into the lust of their flesh. Revelation 21:8 states, "But the cowardly, the unbelieving, the vile, the murders, the sexually immoral, those who practice magic arts, the idolaters and all liars, they will be consigned to the fiery lake of burning sulfur. This is the second death." The burning sulfur is hell.

    The remnants that are rising are people who have the attributes of the Kingdom of God. They are filled with righteousness, peace, and joy in the Holy Spirit according to Romans 14:7. The righteousness they are filled with is of God; it is not their own, this means God finds them in right standing. The peace of God that surpasses all understanding is in them. They have peace that destroys the chaos around them as well as in the world with Christ's authority. They have constant joy, no matter what trial they are facing nor how horrible things may seem in the world. These people know that the joy of the Lord is their strength. These men and women of God are of the Kingdom of God, and they bear these fruits simply because they know their identity. The world doesn't define them, society doesn't define them, nor does their past sins and pains define them. Only God defines them, and they are men and women of prayer. They are always studying God's word to receive fresh revelation and to be renewed so that they can sustain their salvation and fan the flame of the fire God has put in them, which is filled with God's holiness and their temples are a dwelling place for the Holy Spirit and the Glory of God.

    To remain bold, discouragement and fear must be uprooted and defeated. Seeds of discouragement can try to plant in your mind by Satan and his demons to bring you in a place of anxiety and fear. Every vain imagination that shows you a negative outcome of what can happen, and every negative thought that puts you down or in an angry mood is not from God. To be Kingdom people, we must learn to stop this madness of the war in our mind and to not allow these negative thoughts and vain imaginations consume us. This is a strategy of war that the enemy uses against God's people so that they won't have the mind of Christ nor a Kingdom mindset. Job 3:25 states, "For the thing which I greatly feared is come upon me, and that which I greatly feared is come upon me, and that which I was afraid has come unto me." Job was an upright man who God allowed Satan to inflict. However, what came to pass on Job started in his mind. He allowed fear to consume him in his mind and it was birthed to his physical realm. Our words have power in them, power of life or death. Our thoughts have power. What we think and believe can come to pass. This is how people become successful. They begin to see themselves and think of themselves as being successful and it comes to pass. What we think is important, it determines the outcome of our lives. Philippians 4:8 states, "Whatever is noble, whatever is right, whatever is pure, whatever is lovely, whatever is admirable- if anything is excellent or praiseworthy- think about such things." This is the mind of Christ; this is keeping our mind in heavenly places. Kingdom people carry this mindset, and this is why you see success and boldness in what God commissions them to do.

      Having Jesus as your Lord and savior causes you to have the authority to take your mind out of the hands of Satan, and keep it guarded with your helmet of salvation. The helmet of salvation is a part of the armor you receive when you accept Jesus as your Lord and savior (Ephesians 6:10-18); you believe with your heart and confess with your mouth that He is Lord and savior. Christ gives us His authority because he is our covering, we are under his covenant, his protection. Having this knowledge and revelation, you can recite the following scripture when the enemy is trying to fill your mind with negative thoughts like fear.

2 Corinthians 10:5, "Casting down imaginations, and every high thing that exalteth itself against the knowledge of God, and bringing into captivity every thought to the obedience of Christ." Rebuke the negative thoughts in Jesus's name, command them to get out of your mind, then recite the scripture 2 Corinthians 10:5.

There is a mandate for God's kingdom work to be done on this earth. This is the great commission, tell God yes today and go forth into the world and make disciples of all men.

Faith

Hebrews 11:1, "Now faith is the substance of things hoped for, the evidence of things not seen."

Faith is the substance of things hoped for even if you haven't seen it come to pass yet. In order to please God, we must have faith. This means when we are coming before God in prayer and believing in him to move in our lives, we have to believe in our hearts without doubt that He will come through. According to the Oxford Dictionary, doubt is a feeling of uncertainty and as a verb, fear, means to be afraid. Doubt comes from a place of fear. Fear is a spirit that does not come from God. I have heard many sermons and people say that fear drove their faith. I disagree with this statement because we do not want fear to drive any form of faith. Fear comes from Satan, so why would you want Satan to drive you into faith? It is a deception; it will drive you to doubt not faith. The knowledge of this world is foolish, and as followers of Christ, we must obtain our knowledge and understanding from the word of God. 2 Timothy 1:7 states, "For God has not given us a spirit of fear, but of power, love and a sound mind." The fear and doubt you are feeling is not the Spirit of God.

God commands us to be of good courage and to be strong always. This will develop our faith in God to do what he said he would. Deuteronomy 31:6 states, "Be strong and of good courage, fear not, nor be afraid of them, for the Lord thy God, he it is that doth go with thee; he will not fail thee, nor forsake thee." This is God's promise for his children, those who are followers of Christ, those who are found righteous in him. He will not fail us! He promises that he will not fail us. As people are waiting on God to move on their behalf, at first, they have a lot of faith and with excitement they know God will do it. They jump and clap and yell "hallelujah!" Now in the process, they are still waiting for God to do what He said he will do. They are waiting to see the manifestation of prophetic words and prayers. This happens too much in the process, doubt creeps in. When they don't see in the natural the manifestation of the promise, they become full of fear that things are not looking so good for them, and they become uncertain about the power of God in their lives. So, because they don't see it, they believe that they won't receive it. However, faith is the evidence of things unseen. Having faith means that you do not need to have proof and evidence in your natural sight to see what God has for you; to see the money, the debt paid, loved ones saved, favor, and supernatural turn arounds.

You don't have to see it because you are confident in God, you trust in him. Be of good courage because he promises he will not fail you.

In Hebrews chapter 11, it speaks about the persons in the hall of fame of faith. The people that are mentioned are Abel, Enoch, Noah, Abraham, Sarah, Isaac, Jacob, Joseph, Moses, Rahab, Gideon, Barak, Samson, Jephthah, David, Samuel, and the prophets. One thing they all had in common was their faith in God. They all had been through trials and testing; however, they still had faith. Their perspective was not a worldly perspective but a heavenly one. Their minds were minds of God; they had a Kingdom mindset. They understood the promise was for God's Kingdom to be accomplished here on earth as it is in heaven. Having a Kingdom mindset of faith means that you can trust and believe in God with faith to answer your prayers without seeing it naturally. When Jesus was resurrected, he told Thomas, "Blessed are those who believe me and have not seen me" (John 20:29). The good news is this, since you already believe that Jesus is Lord and savior and the son of God, you have faith. You do not need the evidence to see him to believe by faith, you know who he is. Ephesians 2:8 states, "For it is by grace you have been saved, through faith and this is not from yourselves it is a gift from God." God's grace is a gift freely given so that we can be redeemed by his Son, Jesus Christ. It was through faith that we received our salvation, not seeing him. This pleases God.

Therefore, if you already have faith that Jesus is Lord and savior, have faith that he will come through for you. Have faith that the mountains can be removed and thrown into the midst of the sea. Believe that God can move for your situation now! Faith is not later, it is now, and if it is not now, then it is not faith. We have to live a life pleasing and acceptable to God. Being doubtful and full of fear does not please God. The reason is because we are not trusting him. How can God trust us with what we are desiring, and to be used by him if we don't trust him? To be trusted by God, you must sow trust to reap trust. Have faith, repent for being doubtful, and choose to trust God with every part of your life to move now.

The Key of the House of David

Revelation 3:7-8, "And to the angel of Philadelphia write: These things saith that he is holy, he that is true, he that hath the key of David, he that openth, and no man shutteth; and shutteth, and no man openeth; I know thy works, behold, I have set before thee and open door, and no man can shut it, for thou hast a little strength, and hast kept my word, and hast not denied my name."

    Jesus has the authority to open doors before our lives. These open doors are doors of opportunities. These are opportunities that we as servants of the Lord have been praying, fasting, and sowing for. These opportunities take us to a new place of promotion in ministry, business, and different types of areas that we have been waiting to step into. There are prerequisites that we as believers need to meet before Jesus unlocks the doors to us. Being Kingdom minded, we must understand that benefits and blessings are not just freely handed to us. Salvation was a free gift given to us. It is God's grace by faith that we are saved because we believe with our heart and confess with our mouth that Jesus Christ is Lord. This is just the first step, after this, growth needs to happen. There are riches according to the riches of Jesus Christ such as his power, wealth, and success. New levels are a part of our inheritance as servants of God. There is a term that Pastor Glen Anthony used in one of his sermons, "Fan the flame." We must be responsible to fan the flame of the Holy Spirit that was given to us. That means, grow in the Lord, be transformed by His word, meditate on His word, and get around your tribe who will help you grow into the new creation God has made you.

In Revelation 3:7-8, Jesus speaks about the works of the Philadelphia church. The Philadelphia church were a people who held on to God's word, obeyed him, and followed him even though there were challenging times. In those times, it seemed as if they had little strength; however, they kept God's word and they did not deny his name, no matter how trying their life was. The Philadelphia church had a Kingdom mindset. Their eyes were fixed on heaven, and their minds were sound and transformed into the mind of Christ. What they saw with the natural eye did not determine their faith in God. They had such strong faith in God, they were obedient to His word and to His command. Prerequisites of God's word which were to be holy and to be true according to verse 7, were not bothersome to them. John 14:15 states, "If you love me, keep my commandment." The understanding of God's love was revealed to these people through His word. They had fallen in love with God and His word. This only happens when there is a deep desire to fellowship and to get close to God. Studying the Bible is not another school assignment, it is an intimate and beautiful time when the Holy Spirit reveals the secrets and the heart of God. A hunger and thirst for righteousness was increasing on a daily basis because they loved being close to God.

Don't allow the practices and customs of this world to influence you as you wait for the doors to open for your life. A lot of people turn away from God and search to obtain wealth, riches, and success by practicing witchcraft and new age occult practices. It may seem on the surface that what they do and what a believer of Christ does is the same. When we decree a thing, it is established according to Job 22:28; we believe it, see it, and speak it and it comes forth. When seeing and believing, we are tapping into our prophetic imagination which any one can tap into. Romans 11:29 tells us that the gifts of God come without repentance, prophecy is included in this. People turn to card readers and psychics to determine their future because they are foretelling. Prophecy is to encourage, edify, correct, and foretell. The major difference is that correction and edification is included. The blessing of God comes without sorrow. Blessings from the prophetic words of fortunetellers known as soothsayers come with sorrow. They are also tapping into a heavenly realm, but they are entering realms opened up by demonic portals.

Servants of God tap into the heavenly realms, but Jesus is unlocking those portals, doors, and realms. These are safe places that fill us with truth and challenges us to be obedient to God and to grow in Him. Therefore, the open doors and blessings Jesus unlocks are not filled with sorrow. Jeremiah 29:11 states, "For I know the plans I have for you, plans to prosper you, not to harm you…" When Jesus unlocks the door, Satan has no authority to shut it nor stay in the way. Jesus is the only one with the key of David, not a spirit guide nor idol god you worship. They may be opening doors, but they are full of sorrow, emptiness, and disappointments. Our next levels and blessings are available ahead of us in that door that is assigned to us. When we prepare ourselves for what God has for us and are ready, then those doors open up.

Your obedience and faithfulness are keys that also open the doors to your next. Sometimes an opportunity will come to you, but it doesn't mean that opportunity is aligned to your will and purpose in your life. When you surrender to God and align your life to him, he will begin to take away people, places or things in your life that will be in the way of the door you are supposed to see and walk through. That door is a God destined opportunity you've been praying for. It could be a business, career, ministry, and/or relationship. However, if we are distracted with what is not for us, we are delaying what is meant for us. It is the will of God to prosper you and to put you in a position to be laborers for the harvest for God's kingdom here on earth as it is in heaven.

The Potter's Hand

Isaiah 64:8, "But now O Lord, thou art our father; we are the clay and thou our potter we are the work of thy hand."

We are the masterpieces of the work of our Lord's hand. In our sin and iniquities, our vessels were tarnished and made weak, it was not beautiful. The trials of this life, us coming out of God's protection to fulfill our personal desires, the enemy beats us down. Our vessels become shattered and broken. As we gaze upon our broken vessels, we are filled with great regret, shame, and disappointment. Too many times we begin to gather up the broken pieces to put ourselves back together again and fix it. But because we are fixing our vessels on our own, with our own hands, we do not put the vessel together correctly. We have tried fixing ourselves over and over and we forget how we looked before our iniquities came upon us. Identity is lost and oppression fills our vessels, smashing us into pieces once again. This is exactly how we look trying to mold our own life in vain. Everything we try to build and find our worth and identity in just brings disappointment after disappointment. Making many people believe that they are not worthy to follow Jesus and that they have messed up too bad to start all over again.

Start over. Let the vessel shatter to the ground. God does the greatest work for us in our most broken state. The vessel keeps shattering because God needs to get rid of the old vessel to mold you a new one, and you keep trying to put back together broken pieces of old that aren't capable of keeping you and holding you. A potter has the clay in his hand molding a vessel that is pleasing before his sight. His hand is on the vessel, and that is the same with you. God's hand is on you as he shapes you into a pleasing vessel before his eyes. What you are being created into is a new creature in Christ that will be strong, stable, and beautiful.

Allowing God to be the potter in our lives, requires full surrender and submission. This means we have to stop resisting God, and that we must yield to his superiority and authority over our lives. When we call God our Lord, we are saying He is the owner of our lives. People do not yield to God's authority over their life because they want to do what pleases them and respond to God's call when they are ready. When the disciples followed Jesus, they left their jobs, they dropped everything to follow him. I am not saying to quit your job, I am telling you that you must be ready to let go of your old life to follow Jesus. It gets very exhausting when constantly putting your own vessel back together. In time, pieces come up missing, they chip more, and when you put it back together it doesn't look the same. When you have been so far away from God and your heart is far from him, you cannot recognize yourself. Not in physical appearance, but in your character. You must have asked yourself, "What happened to me? This isn't me." There is good news, since you know deep in your heart that the person of sin is not who you are supposed to be, God is pulling your heartstrings towards him. He is calling you back to your first love.

This was the character of the church of Ephesus, and where many people are today. You realize you can't stand evil, and you can recognize who is of God and who isn't. But why do people regress and hold themself up knowing this very thing? Their hearts are far from God, and he wants you to come back to your first love. He is our first love. We left him to pursue people and things of the world just to feel satisfied because we couldn't wait on God's promise for our life. Revelation 2:7-8 states, "Nevertheless, I have this against you, that you have left your first love. Remember therefore from where you have fallen; repent and do the first works, or else I will come to you and remove your lampstand from your place-unless you repent." God is calling his bride into repentance. God is love and he takes us willingly but leaving him he will hold that against us, and we will not enter the Kingdom of heaven.

As Kingdom citizens here on earth, we must not leave our first love which is God. We must abide in him, and he will abide in us. We will be his people and he will be our God. He has to be first in all areas of our lives, that is why we are told in Matthew to seek first the kingdom of God. Sons and daughters of the Kingdom do not resist God's hand, they yield to his authority. We allow God to have his way in us and he mold us into who he wants us to be. It's not our will, but God's will to be done here on earth as it is in heaven. We are being created to be His workmanship according to Ephesians 2:10 We were created in Christ Jesus, not by our own hand and will. This is for good works for the Kingdom of God that need to be done here on earth before Jesus Christ returns. So, we need to walk in his statues, meditate on the word day and night, and allow God to mold us and to be the potter of our lives. God will not be able to use self-willed, selfish people for his Kingdom work because it will taint the work of God. He only uses those who are willing, submitted, and faithful servants to him. Let him be your potter and allow him to mold you. God is the creator of the heavens and the earth; he makes all things beautiful and everything he creates he sees it as good. Look at this world: the stars, the land, the water, and the animals all created by God. If he can make the world in 7 days, imagine what he would do to you in 7 days as you submit to his ways.

So, stop resisting the potter's hand and let him complete the work he started. Allow God to work so that you can have a Kingdom mindset. Become a vessel to do great works for God's Kingdom on this earth so that God can receive the glory and help bring lost souls into his Kingdom.

Don't Become a Pillar of Salt

Genesis 19:24, "Then the Lord rained upon Sodom and upon Gomorrah brimstone and fire from the Lord out of heaven."

We must move forward into God's will to see his Kingdom manifest here on earth, in our lives, homes, businesses, and churches. To move forward, we have to let go of old baggage. The reason you haven't seen any progress and sometimes find yourself regressing into old familiar places and people is because you are still holding on to your past instead of moving into the place God wants to bring you. The word "forward" according to the Oxford Dictionary means, "the direction one is facing; towards the front, onward so as to make progress; toward a successful conclusion, toward the future; ahead in time." Notice in the definition of forward it says to face front, not backwards. How can you make progress to success and move into the future if you are facing backwards? If you are facing back instead of front, you are going to walk right back into your past, into your sins and iniquities. A lot of times people are just looking back, staring at their Sodom and Gomorrah, and are unable to move. They have become stagnant because they turned into a pillar of salt. In Genesis 19:26 it states, "But Lot's wife looked back and she became a pillar of salt." Lot's wife didn't want to let go of where they were instructed to leave because she thought those were the best days. The best days are not in the past, the best days are ahead.

Sodom means to burn, and Gomorrah means ruined. So why would you want to look back and miss a place that was meant to burn and be ruined? We can get all the deliverance we want from soul ties, past hurts, traumas, past pains, you name it. After we get our deliverance, it is up to us to stay free and delivered. Luke 11:24-26 speaks about when an unclean spirit returns. Once it returns and sees that the house is empty and out of order, it brings seven other spirits that are even more evil and they all dwell in that place once again. You get your deliverance, but you are not filling yourself with the Spirit of God. Getting delivered is an opportunity to not dwell and miss the past. Ask the Lord to show you what brought you there, what doors are open in your life, and what you need to do to change so that you never go back! Pray and meditate on God's word, look up scriptures that pertain to your struggles; be it perversion, fornication, insecurity, greed, low self-esteem, fear, et cetera. It is all in the Bible, which is the Word of God. It is a tool that we have access to, to get our full healing, deliverance, and breakthrough. You can also get counseling; counseling is not bad at all, it will help your mental health, and confront what needs to be exposed and dealt with. This will help maintain your freedom.

Move forward into the new beginning God has for you. Isaiah 43:18-19 states, "Remember ye not the former things, neither consider the things of old. Behold, I will do a new thing; now it shall spring forth; shall ye not know it? I will even make a way in the wilderness, and rivers in the desert." Do not be afraid or intimidated of the new paths, God is with you! He is leading you, and he promised that he will make a pathway through the wilderness and create rivers in the dry wasteland. God will create rivers so that you can be healed and made whole, so that you can have access to his living water, and he will also supply all your needs. He did it for the Israelites when they were set free from Egypt. He can do it for you. Take heed and do not complain about the process and the wilderness. Don't desire to go back to what was familiar like the Israelites did which caused a short journey to turn into forty years because God may not take you into the new place if you still have an old mindset, a slave to sin mindset, a limited mindset, a mindset of regression and fear. God will work on you in the wilderness.

A New Mindset

Isaiah 65:17, "For behold, I create a new heaven and a new earth: and the former shall not be remembered or come to mind."

When God creates a new thing, he is creating something that never existed before. A time is coming when this old earth is going to pass away. God is making everything new. That means the old mindset, the old ideas, and the old ways of doing things will no longer be sufficient. It is so exciting that God will do this for his faithful servants. We are being cleansed, prepped, and transformed to enter the new Jerusalem. The first heaven and earth have to pass away; it is full of iniquities, sin, and evil. The ones who will enter eternity are God's people whose names are found in the Lamb's book of life. Esther was prepped before she became Queen. She had to go through a process, and the King found favor in Esther because she was beautiful. To God, his servants who are faithful and pure are beautiful before his eyes. He is not looking at our outer appearance to determine if he will choose us, he is looking inside of us. He is looking at our heart, our character, and our mindset to see if they match Him.

God wants his people to do a new thing on this earth, in this season, before the return of Jesus Christ. People who have a Kingdom mindset and way of living can discern this in their spirit. That is why there is great separation happening, false prophets and leaders are being exposed. Evil is being exposed in the churches, in our governments, and in our families. The exposure is bringing a great separation among the earth. Trials and hardships are bringing out characteristics and exposing who chooses God or who will choose Satan and the world. Rebellion, dark magic, witchcraft, and new age practices have increased dramatically in this time because people are realizing there is another realm to tap into and they are not choosing God's side because change and transformation are required as well as full submission to God. Rebellious people will not enter the new Jerusalem. There is a second death that is coming for those who will choose not to live for God and want to follow their own ways, their selfish lustful desires. Revelation 21:8 says, "But the cowardly, the unbelieving, the vile, the murderers, the sexually immoral those who practice magic arts, the idolaters and all the liars, they will be consigned to the fiery lake if burning sulfur. This is the second death." This is why there are genuine apostles, prophets, evangelists, pastors, and teachers who are proclaiming the gospel with a Spirit of truth. They are crying out to the church, and the world to get things in order and to seek God. The intercessors are praying for revival. The true remnant is rising up.

Matthew 5:17 states, "Beware of false prophets, which come to you in sheep's clothing, but inwardly they are ravening wolves." These are the ones who are giving messages of perversion to God's people; messages sent to derail and take the people in the wrong direction. They are spreading lies saying, "all will enter the kingdom of heaven, you don't have to change, it's okay to sin, and move left when you are supposed to move right." Maturity is vital within the Body of Christ. Maturity has nothing to do with how long you go to church nor how long you have been saved, it has to do with your understanding and your closeness to God in your walk. If you are easily influenced by any teaching, and you do not take the time to study your word, you will be swayed by the false doctrines and messages that are coming forth to you. Ephesians 4:14 states, "Then we will no longer be immature like children. We won't be tossed and blown by every word of new teaching. We will not be influenced when people try to trick us with lies so clever they sound like the truth." These are the adults in Christ: matured, well-seasoned, the people who represent the Kingdom of God. These people do not believe anything that is thrown at them, they have a high level of discernment. The mature can discern what is right and wrong according to Hebrews 5:14. People of a Kingdom mindset, their hunger for studying the word of God increases, it never stops. They want more and they seek more understanding, and they go before the Father to get a new level of understanding of what the word says. They go deeper in their relationship with God, they want to reach higher heights of glory and new encounters with Jesus because they are hungry for God. We get close to God because we love him, and we get a new understanding of how much he loves us. We want to know God more intimately. These are the people God chooses to do his work for His Kingdom here on earth because they live a life of sacrifice, obedience, and praise. Their discernment is sharp, and they are not tricked by any old message even if it sounds nice. Kingdom people understand that the word of God is a double-edged sword designed to pierce the hearts according to Hebrews 4:12. If the message does not give a word of correction or confronts the sins and corruptions of this world so that salvation can be reached on the earth, they know it is not of God. Who is your influence? What are you allowing in your ear gates and eye gates? Who do you follow and receive words and advice from? Your influence has an impact on your decision-making and your mindset! A Kingdom person of God and the person who is evil, you will know them by their fruits according to Matthew 6:17.

  There is a new door opened before everyone in the Body of Christ. A lot of people are not choosing to mature in the things of God, they are complacent and okay with just being saved and going to church and sitting down and hearing the message instead of allowing it to edify them. I saw a vision that there was an open door. I saw a man in a 1950's style jacket with a hat on in a pick-up truck. He was looking to see if any other vehicles were coming before he proceeded forward. There were no cars coming, but he wouldn't move. He was stuck, and it was open right before him. There are people in the church with an old mindset, the old way of thinking, and they have not stepped forward into the new door because they are worried about what may go wrong as they move forward. So, fear is holding them back. It is obvious that the pathway is clear, but it's their mindset. The old mind is full of fear, and the old ways of dealing with life. In this season, new things are ahead, and we cannot waste time wondering what may go wrong. This creates scenarios that are nonexistent because of the vain imagination fear created. God is calling us to move forward and to step into the new without being afraid. Step into the new. Jesus is coming and only a Kingdom mindset will get you through these last days.

Invite Jesus to Supper

Revelation 3:20, "Behold, I stand at the door and knock: if any man hear my voice, and open the door, I will come in to him, and will sup with him, and he with me."

Have you sat and dined with Jesus? God is waiting for Kingdom minded people to sit and dine with his Son. There are many people within the Body of Christ who have accepted Jesus as their savior, and they believe by simply accepting him that they are covered and that nothing more is required of them because Jesus did the work at the cross. Jesus did indeed die for our sins, and he rose again, and the free gift of grace was given to mankind and those who believe. By faith we believe in him and therefore are saved. It does not stop there, because of the cross we have victory in our lives to overcome sin and we have what we need through Jesus to be successful. However, we must take action and pray because in that time of intimacy we experience maturity. It is time to grow up.

In the book of Revelations chapters 2 and 3, Jesus spoke about the 7 churches. These 7 churches are the condition and the state which many people in the Body of Christ are in. The church of Ephesus - cannot bear evil, but they have fallen and forgotten the first works. Jesus is calling this group to come back to their first love with the same passion and same fervency they had when they were saved. The church of Smyrna - the people who have been afflicted and who have gone through tribulation. Their names were slandered by people, those who called themselves Jews, but they really weren't. They are to remain faithful unto death even in times of persecution. The church of Pergamos - people who have not denied their faith, but cling to the teachings of Balaam who taught Balak to set traps and stumbling blocks before the sons of Israel; this means to entice them and give themselves up to sexual vice. The church of Thyatira - known for their love, faith, service, and patience, but they tolerated Jezebel who led the servants away into fornication (sexual vice). Jesus says Jezebel will be thrown into a bed of anguish and those who commit adultery with her (church of Thyatira) and her children will be dead in a strike in a moment. The church of Sardis - the people who are supposed to be alive but are dead; also known as the dead church. These people are called to be strengthened and to come back alive. They need revival. The church of Laodiceans - people who are lukewarm, they have one foot in the world and one foot in the church. They cannot make up their mind on what direction to go. They are still being led by the flesh, but their Spirits are desiring God.

Examine your heart, which church do you fall under? The Spirit of Perversion has entered the churches as well as fear. The gospel is being perverted. There are Pastors leading sheep astray and there are people who do not realize that they are being led astray according to Jeremiah 50:6. They're being led to hell. I encourage every lost soul to come as they are, but do not end it there. This walk with Christ is not made for the weak, the dead, the lukewarm, the sexual immoral. You're coming to Christ with the mindset that you are turning away from your sins which means to repent and have your mind renewed and allow the gospel to transform them a 180-degree turn. Say a prayer of repentance to denounce sins and be filled with the Holy Spirit. Once you have an encounter with the Holy Spirit there is no way you will regress. A very important step to take is getting deliverance. There is deliverance that needs to take place to deliver these people of past hurts, trauma, and generational curses. I encourage counseling because it will help maintain deliverance, to be healed and whole. Find a Christian counselor who understands deliverance. They are out there!

Jesus is knocking on the doors of unbelievers, the misled, and the confused. A great spirit of revival is beginning to sweep the nations and the churches, and the ones who receive it are the ones that desire it. You have to want it. In Revelation 3:20, Jesus says that he will come in and eat with him and he with him. This is breaking bread, the same that the apostles did fellowshipping with other brethren. Just like we break bread and fellowship with our local church that God has called us to serve in and to be covered by Jesus wants to do this very thing with us; fellowship, break bread, and commune with us. Jesus wants to talk with us, and he wants us to talk with him. This is when we pour out our concerns and talk about the good and the bad with Jesus. Abraham's righteousness led him to be a friend of God. We are being led to live a holy and righteous life so that we can be able to commune with Jesus. Jesus is our faithful friend, and he wants the same faithfulness to be poured back into him. The blessing of the Lord is upon the faithful ones. Remain in him and he will remain in you. Open the door of your whole heart; your pain, past, trauma, hurt, and the good times … all of it! Will you invite Jesus to sit and eat with you?

Communion

1 Corinthians 11:23, "For I have received from the Lord that which also I delivered unto you, The Lord Jesus the same night in which he was betrayed took bread."

The word "betray" in Greek is "paradidomi" which means "up to give or deliver over." In the Oxford Dictionary, betray means "to expose one's country, group or person to danger by treacherously giving information to an enemy also known as treason." When Jesus broke bread with the disciples during the last supper he had with them, while his betrayal was in progress, he told them that the bread was his body which was broken for them (us). To break something is to separate it and/or crush it. Jesus was willing to become broken to cover the broken state of mankind so that we can be forgiven and become healed and whole. Jesus was captured when this happened, but he told the disciples that his body was broken for them. He knew that the time was coming to drink of the cup, and they drank from the cup that represented His blood in remembrance of him. Then in Gethsemane he drank from the cup, again yielding to the Father's authority and the plan to die for us. Someone who may not be a believer may question, "Why would Jesus want us to remember his death when he rose again and came back to life like the Bible claims?" We do this as a worship to the Lord, remembering what he did during the good times and bad times. Many of us have encountered bad times such as betrayal. Judas betrayed Jesus, but Jesus didn't curse him. Jesus told him to go and do what he needed to do. Jesus understood that betrayal was a pathway into the promise. This world is full of sin and people betray and backstab people all the time, it is a fallen world. Jesus had already forgiven Judas. When we take communion, we take it with no unforgiveness or hate against anyone in our heart because if we do, we are guilty of the bloodshed of the Lord's body. Judas betrayed Jesus and killed himself because of the guilt. He was so consumed in evil thoughts that he missed the fact that Jesus sacrificed for him to be saved too.

How many times have you been betrayed? Who were or are the Judases in your life that you have encountered? What is your perspective towards the Judases in your lifetime? Are you angry, full of bitterness, and/or are you hurt? Jesus didn't beg Judas to stay with him and to not betray him because he knew that Judas had to do it. Jesus released Judas knowing about the betrayal. To become Kingdom minded on this earth, we have to release Judas from our minds and hearts. Too many people are taking communion, still holding on to the hurt of those who have betrayed them and left them for dead. We are causing ourselves to be guilty of the blood that Jesus shed instead of being cleansed from it. This is why it is so hard for so many people to move on and grow up in Christ. We are called to be like Christ. Look at how Jesus handled Judas. He released him and when Judas came with the soldiers to have him arrested, Jesus called him friend and asked why he was there? I believe Jesus was giving him an opportunity to talk with him like he wants to do with all of us. The point that I am making is that Jesus didn't lose his character. Jesus stood in his sonship authority and who He is. He didn't allow betrayal, people, nor the crucifixion to move him because He came to die for people just like them. The action here is that Jesus released and didn't condemn Judas. Just like in the Lord's supper, when we come together, we don't come together to condemn but to be judged by the Lord, to be chastened, and to be disciplined. Jesus was disciplined the entire time of his betrayal and crucifixion. He saw what was ahead; beyond the cross, the tearing of the veil, when he came back and ascended, and left the Holy Spirit. When all the apostles were going out into the world to make disciples, baptizing them in the name of the Father, Son, and Holy Spirit. He saw you. He saw you surrendering your life to him and being willing to do anything to spread the gospel and to live for him. Spread out the message of hope and good news to all the world. Jesus saw that not our sins, not when we betrayed him and fell away. His blood covered that.

Jesus came to remove the veil in the temple so that we could have access to God's throne through him. Jesus had to be betrayed. After he was beaten and his body became broken, he died for us, and he rose up out of the grave! Our mind and soul have to be broken, separated, and crushed! The anointing comes from the pressing and the crushing. During the crushing and death, Jesus took the keys of death from hell which removed the sting of death from the faithful servants who believe in him and follow his way. Jesus was crushed and put to death to bring the anointing of the resurrection power. God is breaking the Body of Christ from old mindsets and old ways of being so that we can die to our flesh. He is breaking those aspects of ourselves so that we can have rule over the death of our flesh. When we have more power, our flesh has to yield to the Spirit inside of us. We become a new creature in Christ, transformed by the word of God so that we can be resurrected as Kingdom people.

Teach These Fingers to War

Not by Might nor by Power...
The Spirit God

1 Samuel 17:37, "David said moreover, The Lord that delivered me out of the paw of the lion, and out the paw of the bear, he will deliver me out of the hand of the Philistine, And Saul said unto David, Go, and the Lord be with thee."

The stone of David's sling shot didn't kill Goliath, his faith in God did. To be a warrior, a force to be reckoned with in spiritual warfare against Satan and his kingdom, there are important attributes we must have. David was known as a mighty valiant man and a man of war who was prudent in matters and a comely person. David was valiant, known as showing courage, because he never backed down from a fight. He slew a lion and a bear that went after the sheep he was attending; he protected his flock. A Shepherd (a Pastor) does not leave their flock (the church) for dead when danger comes, he protects them and with courage takes down the lion and the bear. David was a man of war during his youth and also when he led the Israelites to war later down the line; he was known for his victories. David was a prudent man, which also means showing care for thought of the future. David never left the sheep unattended. When Samuel was seeking to anoint the next king of Israel from Jesse's house, David was not there, he was out attending to the sheep because he cared for them, and they were his first assignment. Even when his father Jesse sent him to bring lunch to his brothers, he left a keeper with the sheep; he didn't just leave the sheep wandering. We can learn a lot from David; faithfulness, consistency, and mastering your assignment even if it is low level because you cannot elevate until you operate in your current assignment with excellence. David was a comely person; he was suitable and pleasant looking. Beauty comes from inside out. There may be people who may appear pleasant, but their heart and character are hideous and wicked which makes them unattractive. David was a man after God's heart, he loved to worship Him, he lived for Him, and most importantly he fought for Him. This beauty of his heart was seen outwardly. God's face shines upon us when we are constantly in his presence and in communion with him.

    A valiant warrior and a man of war has courage and does not fear in battle. Fear is an emotion caused by a belief. To be fearful of spiritual warfare and engaging in it, you have entered into the battle with a defeated mindset. You allow your emotion of fear to take you away from the victory. Usually, it starts out with a thought, "What if this? What if that? What if I lose? What if I don't get my breakthrough? What if my money runs out?

What if they don't like me? What if I fail?" These thoughts create emotional fear. When you are not operating in the anointing, when engaging in spiritual warfare, you are full of nothing but fear. There are battles that we as intercessors are assigned and called to. The battles that we are called to, God will anoint us for them. The battles that we are not called to, there is no anointing, and the fight is done in our own strength, not that of the Holy Spirit. The Holy Spirit is known as counselor, helper, advocate, and intercessor. The battle you are called to, the Holy Spirit will guide you and be by your side, back you up, and intercede on your behalf. While you are obeying God in the assignments he gives you, and you are fighting the battles, the Holy Spirit is there telling you what scripture to use during the warfare, telling you what we need to pray for and against, what to bind and what to loose, and he intercedes before God letting him know if we are weary, if we need assistance, if we need rest and if more ground is being covered, taken, and if battles are won in victory. There are levels when it comes to warfare. In the class, Accessing the Anointing by Simple Truth LLC created by Bishop H.R Crump and Overseer Kheona Crump, it was stated that David's anointing was in levels. The first level was tending the sheep, then upgraded to killing the lion, upgraded to killing the bear, and then taking down Goliath. One point they made was that David didn't go from tending sheep to Goliath, there were battles in between that he had to step into in order to be promoted to the next level. These levels you are anointed for, and you must master the smaller battles before stepping into the bigger one. Mastering the battles, David was not in fear and his confidence and courage grew. Therefore, he knew he could conquer the next thing and he was so bold in it, this caused him to be valiant and a man of war.

Prudence is a trait of a warrior. This means we show care for all we do and whoever and whatever group we are assigned to. We are not reckless and selfish. Going into battles, it's not only for us all the time, but also to cover our Pastors, leaders, churches, families, and our territories. If you do not care for the needs of others and for this world, there is no victory in the battle. David was a successful man of war because of his prudence. He allowed God to lead him in every battle and he protected his sheep; he didn't allow danger to the flock, and he never left them unattended even when he went to give lunch to his brothers during the battle of the Philistines. This trait took David to the assignment that would forever change his life. He went up against Goliath and took him down with his slingshot and stone. King Saul at the time could see that the Lord was with David and told him to go fight Goliath even though his brothers didn't believe in him. He was comely because of his courage and his heart for God was so clear for all to see. He was angry when the Philistine giant was cursing God. When you love someone, you fight for them and you will not allow anyone or anything to speak against them or attempt to destroy them, and if you need to fight you will fight. The Goliaths, standing against our God in our nations, territories, homes, churches, and Pastors should get you angry because a Kingdom-minded warrior fights for the Kingdom of God here on earth. We don't sit back defeated and let the enemy kill, steal, and destroy us.

    Our faith brings victory. David's faith in God brought down Goliath, a small stone compared to a giant alone doesn't kill it, our faith in God does. If God is for us, and the Holy Spirit is backing us up and we are anointed for this, the giants are coming down! God was moved by David's heart, he had to back him up and give Holy Ghost power to that stone. He had assistance to take the giant down, the anointing gave him the ability to do in the natural what no one else could do. No one could take down Goliath, they weren't anointed for it, they weren't anointed to be the next King of Israel, their hearts weren't for God. David was chosen, he was picked, he was qualified, and the favor of God was with him because he never went to battle without Him.

A Cup of Water

2 Samuel 23:15, "And David longed, and said, Oh that one would give me a drink of water from the well of Bethlehem, which is by the gate. And the three mighty men broke through the host of the Philistines and drew water out of the well of Bethlehem and brought it to David; nevertheless he would drink not thereof, but poured it out unto the Lord."

During the war with the Philistines in 2 Samuel 23, three of David's mightiest warriors, went down to meet David during harvest time to the cave of Adullam while the Philistines pitched in the valley of Rephaim. David was in the hold and the garrison of the Philistines was then in Bethlehem. David longed for a drink of the water from the well in Bethlehem. The three mighty men went and broke the lines of the Philistines and fought to get David a drink of water. These three men were valiant just like David. They had courage and didn't fear anything, they believed in their leader David, and they trusted in him because he brought them to victory every time. They had victory because David sought after God, and he wouldn't move without His instructions and without Him. David depended on God for the victory, he depended on the move of the Spirit. He wouldn't move out of order like Saul did. David had an understanding that God's ways are higher, and he experienced victory because of his faithful obedience to God's direction.

David was sowing obedience, trust, and faithfulness in God in all that he did. Even during the first assignment of tending the sheep, to the lion, the bear, Goliath, the trial when Saul wanted to kill him and caused him to hide, and then as King of Israel. David reaped a benefit because of this, he had three mighty men who would fight and stand by his side no matter what. They had trust in David because of their track record of victory because David led the troops. Their devotion was so deep to David, they were willing to fight where the Philistines were taking camp so that David could have the water from the well of Bethlehem he longed for. In 2 Samuel 23:14, David didn't order the three men to get him water, he just expressed one of his longings during this battle. As a warrior, what are you sowing into the Spirit of God (into God)? Are you faithful and obedient? Do you trust God to lead you so that you can have the victory? The next question to ponder on is, who are you connected to? Your prayer partners, your friends, are they faithful and devoted and ready to fight with you? If not, have you been faithful to the assignments God has called you to? Are you obedient to your Pastors and leaders, and what they ask of you? There is a sowing and reaping principle, but also who we are connected to determines how far we are going. There are people who are God assigned and sometimes people write them off because of their appearance. God didn't pick the King of Israel out of appearance, but what was in his heart. The quietest person can be a giant in the Spirit. We are to look at a man's heart, not their appearance. Don't write off the godsends for what you want, because the godsends will fight for you and the ones you pick usually do not care about you at all. There are so many branches when it comes to connection with people. We are who we attract as well. Who are you? Are you obedient, faithful, and trusting? Does God see those things in you? Those attributes are needed so that God can trust you with the anointing to be a warrior and glory carrier on this earth.

    David poured out the water from the well of Bethlehem instead of drinking it. He was so moved by the three mighty men's devotion towards him, he wanted to pour the water to give it to the Lord. Honor the Lord, give honor to where honor is due. David explained that the cup of water was their life blood; they risked their lives to get it for him and he refused to drink it. To David, it would have been like drinking the life blood of the mighty men. The sacrifice of putting their lives on the line had to be offered as an offering or a gift to God. David understood that he was not worthy to drink the cup, he was not an equal to Him

(God). David had a heart of servitude to the Father, and he never moved outside of God's will. For this very reason, David was successful, and God was always with him. David was grateful for the mighty men's devotion to him, but this also taught them that David doesn't get the glory, God gets the glory. David had to teach them that God leads them to victory, not him. So, David, in the sight of men, humbled himself before God to give honor to where honor was due.

I believe that David recognized God's gift in his life, the Israelites' life, and the life of generations to come. In John 4, the Samaritan woman was drawing water from the well of Jacob. When Jesus asked her for a drink of water, she was puzzled that he would talk to a Samaritan seeing that he was a Jew. John 4:10 states, "Jesus answered and said to her, 'If you knew the gift of God, and who it is who says to you, 'Give Me a drink,' you would have asked Him, and He would have given you living water.'" Jesus tells the woman that if she would have recognized Him that she would have asked Him for a drink that He would have given her living water. David himself was prophetic, his music and his prayers were prophetic as well as his actions, being that Jesus came from the bloodline of David. Not only wouldn't David drink the cup the mighty men brought to him, but in his devotion to God he gave the drink to God as an offering; this can also represent that only God could quench his thirst. Not a physical thirst, but his spiritual thirst. God filled him, lifted him up, ministered to him, set him free, forgave him, and delivered him from evil. David's life shows how much God was pleased with him and loved him because his heart was towards God.

Only God quenches our spiritual thirst. To be a warrior for the Kingdom of God, we don't look for the water of the well to satisfy us; our satisfaction is in God. A true warrior of Christ that leads others, will never allow their title or position to make themselves more superior than God to people who are following them. A leader will show the other warriors following him/her that God is leading them and bringing them to victory. When the leader is given honor and devotion, the leader will give it as an offering to God so that He can get all the glory. The reason for doing this is simple: the leader recognizes God's gift and that what He has to offer is better than precious silver, gold, and the water of this world. God gives us living water so we will never thirst again, and we are strengthened and rejuvenated for the battle.

The Lord's Anointed

1 Samuel 24:10 "Look, this day your eyes have seen that the Lord delivered you today into my hand in the cave, and *someone* urged *me* to kill you. But *my eye* spared you, and I said, 'I will not stretch out my hand against my lord, for he *is* the Lord's anointed.'"

To be anointed is to be consecrated and set apart. To be anointed also means to be divinely appointed. Saul was divinely appointed to be the King of Israel. Saul anointed David to be the next King because the Lord stripped Saul's authority, according to 1 Samuel 15:27, because of his disobedience and him rejecting the Lord's policies and directions. David was chosen because of his heart towards God. Saul was selected originally from the people of Israel because they wanted a king. They had a carnal mindset and couldn't recognize the King was in heaven. So, they chose Saul based on his appearance. God chose David based on his heart, not his appearance. A good leader knows how to be a good follower. This means following commands and directions as well as having an obedient heart and a heart to serve.

Saul grew jealous of David. God sent the same evil spirit upon him that he sent when he learned that His family's bloodline would not rule over Israel. The evil spirit tormented Saul and only David playing the harp soothed him. David was the Lord's anointed one; in his music, serving, and victory in the battles against the Philistines proved that the Lord was with him. Even Saul recognized this because he once knew what it was like to have God's favor and to have God as an advocate for him because he no longer had that. I believe Saul could tell when someone had the Lord's favor. Saul made David an armor bearer because he needed to have a connection with God's favor somehow. Seeing how mighty David had become as a man of war and how David killed 10,000 Philistines while Saul only killed 1,000, jealousy and the evil spirit came upon Saul. God was the one who placed the evil spirit because Saul was rebellious and selfish. David's heart sought God; he was prudent in his ways. Even though he had orders and duties placed on him by his father Jessie and King Saul, he willingly followed and obeyed. God saw that and knew David could be the carrier of the anointing to be King of Israel. When David became King, he also was the priest. Saul was not a priest; he was more arrogant because of his position as a King. That's why he felt he could do the animal sacrifice that only priests can do and move ahead out of battle. Saul was a King, but he didn't have a heart that served, he couldn't measure up to be a priest before God, he was only a king for the people.

When placed in a leadership position in ministry we are called to serve the people, not gloat and/or force people to follow because of a title. We are serving according to the ministry or office we are placed in to help edify, exhort, and grow the body of Christ in its walk with Christ, gifting, and talents. As a leader or follower, we must honor and respect the Lord's anointed ones: our Overseers, Pastors, Ministry leaders. We honor and respect them by serving them to whatever capacity plus more. Even if our leaders are having an off day; meaning they are moody, tired, and/or acting out in a manner that is not usual, we shouldn't get upset and badger them, we serve them and do exactly what they need to make the load easier for them. Hebrews 13:17 states, "Obey your spiritual leaders, and do what they say. Their work is to watch over your souls, and they are accountable to God. Give them reason to do this with joy and not with sorrow. They would certainly not be for your benefit." Our spiritual leaders give an account for our souls before God. So, when they correct us, say no to us, and ask us to serve in an area that needs help, we should be joyful and willing to help and serve them because it takes the whole team, organization, church, and the Body of Christ to successfully complete assignments and missions.

There are other forms of authority that God places in our lives separate from our Spiritual leaders. We have governing authority which some include the President, senates, judges, local government leaders, and law enforcement. A lot of believers feel as if they do not need to submit to such officials because of the slander that has come upon those people from the media and bad mouthing. Romans 13:1 states, "Everyone must submit to governing authorities. For all authority comes from God, and those in positions of authority have been placed there by God." Those people are placed there by God, whether their purpose was to do good or evil, because God's will for the world has to come to pass. God will allow certain individuals to be in those positions. Israel wanted a king and picked Saul. God allowed him to be King even though he knew Saul's fate and what was to come. The flaw of our governments and people shows there is only one King that we look to and he is in Heaven. If there are treacherous laws passed against the church, and laws that would compromise our morals and commandments from the Bible, then we are to stand on the Word. This is when we believe for God to make a way for us like he did with David. Saul was after David, but God never allowed Saul to have David in his hand. David was protected and with him the whole time because he was led by the Spirit of God which made him a successful man of war. Cover those leaders in prayer for their salvation and deliverance and that they make decisions based on the leading of the Holy Spirit. No matter what, remain in God and trust Him.

David understood that he had to submit to authority. King Saul was his king, and the relationship they had, Saul addressed David as son and David addressed him as father. This shows the closeness of the relationship the two had before Saul grew jealous and wanted to kill David. David was more successful in battle than Saul, he could have fought back and killed Saul whenever he wanted to. He knew he was to become king of Israel. David could have convinced the people to choose him and when Saul was in his reach David could have killed him. Saul couldn't see him, and it would have been an easy kill. The fact that David didn't do none of this, showed his character. His character was known to be a valiant man and a man of war who was prudent and comely. In other words, he was not a coward and he cared about what was ahead for the future. That is what it means to be prudent. David knew that what he sowed, he would reap as King of Israel when it was his time. David was not perfect, and he had his own shortcomings and falls, but his heart pleased God. It is a cowardly move to kill someone behind their back. A man of war and honor didn't cheat to have victories nor to move ahead out of their own selfish desires. That was not a part of who David was. There was no way David could've killed Saul because he loved Saul and called him father. To add to that, David honored Saul as the Lord's anointed. Saul was not after God, he rebelled against Him, he didn't honor the Prophet Samuel's words, and his loyalty was to himself. If Saul could turn away from God very easily for his own selfish ambition, he could have easily turned on those who were close to him, loved him, and honored him.

David had a Kingdom mindset. Going to battle against Goliath, he went to take him down because Goliath was defiling God. David wouldn't kill Saul because he understood and took to heart to honor authority and to not touch the Lord's anointed. His motives behind these moves were to honor God and to not turn against God. There is a difference when someone is under manipulative leadership and it's an unhealthy relationship. Even so, you honor that leader until the Lord shows you a way out. God will not allow His righteous ones to be put to shame and He will always make a way during times of inflictions and attacks from someone who has an evil spirit on them. Though a bad leader may try to curse you, as long as you follow David's example and what the Word says, "to bless those that curse you" (Luke 6:28), that curse will not have an effect on you. You are remaining in right standing before God and God will honor that. There are great leaders who God has anointed and have fallen short. We are called to not condemn them but to pray for them. Cover your leaders so that witchcraft, sin, sickness, and any attack of the enemy doesn't come up against them. In war, when you take a leader out, you can take the whole team down. So, we must as warriors and watchmen stay on post to make sure these attacks do not come to take our leaders down. When someone or something is assigned against our leaders, you have to remember it is to come against God. That is defiling God, so we must be courageous and strong to tear down every Goliath rising up against our leaders, churches, families, and home. Millennial Warrior, intercessor, watchman, you are anointed for this. Honor your leaders no matter what! Cover them in prayer and take down any force of darkness that dares to rise up against them. Be strong and of good courage. God will go with you wherever you will go, even in battle.

How the Mighty Have Fallen

2 Samuel 1:27, "How have the mighty have fallen and the weapons of war perished."

There was a battle and Jonathan, Saul's son who was David's best friend, was killed in the battle. Saul laid on his own sword and told an Amalekite to kill him. This was the same person who brought Saul's crown and bracelet to David. David did not rejoice even though he knew he was the next king of Israel. David was anointed to become king in his youth. David was a prudent man. It didn't matter what previously happened between him and Saul, David lamented and fasted after the death of Saul and Jonathan. David smote the Amalekite who killed Saul because he touched the Lord's anointed, and he was an enemy to Israel. David couldn't trust an enemy of Israel and as the new King of Israel he had to teach the people to honor their authority.

David, as King, had a responsibility not only to just rule over the people but to teach them what was moral and immoral. He didn't hold on to a grudge after Saul wanted to kill him. David was obedient to God's directions and instructions. He understood the importance of honoring authority. Abner took

Saul's son, Ishboshath, to be King of Israel knowing David was the next appointed king. This resulted in the division of the Kingdom into the Northern and Southern Kingdom. David was going to take over the land of Judah where he was first crowned King over. David didn't overtake the land without God. The Lord was with David because he never moved into battle without His support. Those who are anointed to do the work of God, here on this earth, need the backing of the Holy Spirit. God will anoint and appoint people; it is up to us as his vessels to maintain that anointing by keeping it fresh. The anointing stays fresh because we have an intimate relationship with the Holy Spirit. The Holy Spirit is there to back us, teach us, and guide us. The anointing is given by God, it is not our own. Even though we can do an assignment because we are anointed, it doesn't mean that we have the authority to move without God. Abner was one of Saul's mighty men who attempted to take the kingdom back into Saul's bloodline. He could have been appointed to gain victory for Israel under Saul's leadership, but that season was over. So, because the Lord was not with them, they grew weak in battle. It is very critical to always make sure as people of God, whatever assignment we step into, we honor our leadership always and have the Lord's support.

David and his men were successful in overtaking the house of Saul because he was anointed and appointed for this season to rule over the people of Israel. Abner had a change of heart and decided to help David become King because of being accused of sleeping with one of Saul's concubines which angered him immensely. Even though Abner changed his mind, he didn't move in an honorable way towards Ishbosheth. Ishbosheth wasn't anointed to be King, but Abner made him King and that was his authority over him. His motive was vengeance. We reap what we sow. Joab then killed Abner because he killed his brother during the battle between the two kingdoms. Abner moved in vengeance and had that same thing coming for him. Honor your leadership no matter what because they are appointed over you. Therefore, pray for them; they are human and need the blood of Jesus as protection and God's leading being seated in a place of authority.

    David lamented for Abner because Abner's death was unjust. He did not want to have unclean blood in his bloodline nor rulership over Israel. David had broken the cycle of dishonoring authority in Israel. His bloodline and rulership had to be pure and righteous. Being anointed means that we break every generational curse and toxic cycles designed to keep us unclean. If our bloodline and our blood is unclean, we hinder and block the anointing over our lives and assignments. You can also block your anointing by dishonoring leadership. This kind of leadership includes: a wife to her husband, children to their parents, church members to their Pastor(s), students to their teachers, citizens to governmental leaders. We are called to honor authority in all areas and break the cycle of disobedience and dishonor that has been in our bloodline and our region for many years. We have to pray over our land, because within the United States and all countries around the world, there has been a diabolic need to be the leader and overtake land with war. As people of God, we are Kingdom minded and we break all toxic cycles, and we honor our leadership as to not hinder the anointing for our assignments and in our lives.

Who Am I?

Teach these fingers how to War - How can I rescue Israel?

Judges 6:15, "'But Lord,' Gideon replied, 'how can I rescue Israel? My clan is the weakest in the whole tribe of Manasseh, and I am the least in my entire family!'"

Gideon was chosen to take down the Midianites. Israel was given over to the Midianites because of the evil they committed. They were worshiping the god of Baal instead of God. Baal was known to be a fertility god, which means they counted on this god to bring growth and fertility in the land and among them. This also included perverse sexual orgies and sexual immorality as well as sacrificing babies and humans to this god as worship. This was very wicked before God because God had taken Israel out of Egypt from the hands of Pharaoh. They were stripped of everything instead of being a fertile and fruitful people, and after their rebellious ways they called out to God. God had a covenant with Israel because of Abraham, and he remembered them, and he used Gideon to rescue them. They no longer believed and trusted in God and turned to Baal, so He gave them into the hands of the Midianites, their enemies. The

Midianites took away all they had and stripped them naked. It was so horrible that they had to hide from them. Where was their god of Baal to help them then? They had to be stripped naked after committing all this wickedness to realize that their help didn't come from the hills where sacrifices were made to the god of Baal, but to God who is the maker of heaven and the earth. Does this sound familiar in your own life? Turning away from God to appease your flesh and searching the world to help you because you failed to realize how God has been for you your entire life? Are you willing to be the one in your generation to arise, even if you think you are not qualified?

Gideon considered himself the least of his entire family, but God considered him the greatest. Jesus said in Mark 9:35, "Anyone who wants to be the first must be the very last, and the servant of all." Jesus told this to his disciples after they were arguing on the road about who was the greatest among them. Jesus further explained the heart of serving the people. The fifth law of the "21 Irrefutable Laws of Leadership" by John C. Maxwell is "The Law of Addition." The Law of Addition is that you add value to others by serving them. We add value to a team and ministry by serving the people. Being a leader is not about a position or title, but rather about someone who is able to help the people become more valuable. God saw this quality in Gideon. Notice how he was hiding the grain from the Midianites so that the people could have food. He had a heart of servitude and the fact that he did not hide to do this was an act of courage. A lot of times, people think a small task or assignment doesn't mean much because it is small. "It is the small acts of obedience that leads us to bigger assignments" (Bishop H.R. Crump from the Anointing class in Simple Truth LLC). Little did Gideon know God chose him to lead the Israelites into victory after they cried out to God for help. Gideon's clan was considered the weakest, but they were the strongest. Only 300 men were chosen to go into the battle because they drank water from the cup of their hands and the other thousands were drinking water like dogs. It is not always about the quantity of the people to accomplish a task, it's about the quality. This alone showed the mindset and behavior the people adopted when they turned away from God and worshiped the god of Baal of the Midianites. Gideon had the attributes to lead only three hundred men into battle and he added value to them to become victorious with the Lord's support.

    Gideon performed another act of courage that moved God, he removed the altar of the sacrifice of Baal and replaced it with an altar of sacrifice to God. Gideon didn't hesitate nor did he argue with God, he followed through. This was another assignment Gideon had to complete before being sent out to take power away from the Midianites. God will test our faithfulness to see if we are willing to remove idols or anything that would hinder God's favor and He will give us the push we need to move forward. The people were angry, and they wanted to go after Gideon; however, his father defended him and challenged the people. He told them that since they were angry for what he did against Baal, then Baal would destroy Gideon. They didn't pursue him at all, and they obviously knew that Baal didn't touch him. The Lord was with Gideon; he was anointed, and he was called a mighty man of valor.

A mighty person of valor, a warrior, and a disciple of Jesus is a person of courage and humility. The purpose of leading others into battles against the force of darkness is not for self-gain or self-recognition. It is to build others up and to add value to them when everyone else says that they are weak and unqualified. We have to be courageous enough to tear down idols and to speak the gospel of Christ to remove blinders and to come against the spirit of deception. This spirit of deception is blinding the people and leading them to an unfulfilled life of misery away from God. Not all people will agree with your methods of warfare, prayer, teachings, and techniques. That doesn't mean that you are to allow those smallminded voices to stop you. They are simply distractions. Speak the truth which may seem unpopular to this world. The truth is not going to tickle the ears of the people. The words we speak which are the Word of God are sharper than a double-edged sword. The word is supposed to judge the thoughts and attitudes of the heart of a person. This is used to set the captive free. Rise and shine and allow the Lord to use you to set your generation, and the generations to come, free.

Mighty Warrior

Judges 6:12, "When the angel of the Lord appeared to Gideon, he said, 'The Lord is with you, mighty warrior.'"

How could Gideon be courageous and scared at the same time? To be courageous means to do something that frightens oneself. Gideon took down the altar of Baal, he obeyed God but did it at night because he was afraid to be seen. Many would not have believed this to be courageous. However, you are bold, and it doesn't matter who sees you nor does it matter what people may think. There are many reasons Gideon had to be afraid. One reason was because they were given into the hands of the Midianites; God gave them over to the Midianites due to disobedience and idol worship. God was not with them; they lost everything, and they were stripped to the point of being naked. Another reason was because of how wicked the people of Israel had become. Before I learned about the god of Baal, I first envisioned a group of people bowing to a statue and giving an animal sacrifice and singing weird songs; however, that was not the case. The different pagan gods the Israelites worshiped throughout the years were many, for example, Baal, Ishtar,

Dagon, etc. Some were male or female deities, and they were set up according to the culture and traditions of the people. One main characteristic all these gods had were gods of fertility and growth. To honor these gods, they offered human sacrifices such as babies, there were perverse acts of sexual immorality towards humans and animals, they were full of violence, and people who were out of their right mind caught up in the sins and iniquities blinded by their own lusts. It took for the Israelites to be stripped to nothing to realize that they needed to cry out to the God of their ancestors. Anyone could understand why Gideon was afraid, but that did not stop him from obeying God.

    A lot of times when reading Judges 6, it may seem like Gideon was uncertain that God was with him. It was a shock to him for the Angel of the Lord to appear to him under the oak in Ophrah, commissioning him to lead the people of Israel into victory. Though it may have seemed that all of the Israelites were on Baal's side, that was not the case. Before Gideon and the men went to fight in the battle against the Midianites, God addressed Gideon and told him that there were too many men and that He wanted the number of people in battle to drop. So, Gideon told the men who were afraid to leave. Only 22 men left, but God still knew that there were men who were not fit for the battle. So, He told Gideon to take them to a river and the ones who drank the water like dogs were to leave and the ones who drank the water with cupped hands were the ones called for the battle. Only three hundred men in total cupped their hands to drink the water. God wanted to make sure that He received all the glory for the defeat of the Midianites. Only a few were equipped and still in their right mind to fight on God's behalf. This showed that there were people who were not given over to Baal because God already knew who could fight alongside Gideon for God's glory. I'm sure the prayers of those whose hearts were still after God, were the cries of help He heard. Proverbs 15:29 says, "The Lord is far from the wicked, but hears the prayers of the righteous."

The good news is this mighty warrior, God hears your prayers! Our land may be filled with wickedness, but God hears our cries. His heart is moved by those who intercede on behalf of people and nations. As people who are called to intercede and war in the spirit, we have the authority to speak into situations and see God move. There are prayer warriors out there, who feel like Gideon; they are the least of their family, church, and friends. There are prayer warriors who are still not confident in God because they have experienced what it is like to be far from God and they do not feel qualified because of where they come from or their past. I encourage you with this word, "the first shall be the last and the last shall be the first," you are redeemed through Christ and live for Him. That means you are pursuing a lifestyle of holiness and righteousness, and God hears the prayers of the righteous. I break the lie and curse spoken over you that says that "you are not good enough" or that "you amount to nothing" in Jesus's name. The Lord is with you, go take the territory out of the enemy's hands.

Humility

Judges 8:23, "And Gideon said unto them, I will not rule over you, neither shall my son rule over you: the Lord shall rule over you."

    Gideon led three hundred men to destroy the Midianites. God used Gideon in a powerful way to go after the kings and princes of the Midianites and overthrow their army. The three hundred men blew trumpets, broke pitchers, and held lamps in their hands. A great fear arose within the camp and the army of the Midianites began to flee. Three hundred men of Israel pursued them to overtake them. Gideon was able to capture the princes and he slew them. Gideon also captured the kings. Gideon went back to the men of Succoth who refused to feed him and his army bread when they were weary. With thorns and briers, they taught them a lesson and tore down the tower of Penuel. Even the kings wanted Gideon to slay them after his oldest son couldn't because he was only a youth. With only three hundred men, the Midianites were overthrown, and all the people once again feared the God of Israel. Gideon who was considered the least of his family was the highest of them all, he was a noble man who was sure to give God the glory.

    The Israelites still failed to see that God rescued them. They requested that Gideon and his son and son's son rule over them. After all the battles and energy used to rescue the Israelites, I could only imagine the disgust Gideon must have felt due to the history of whoring over other gods and idols other than God. Gideon didn't turn down a position of leadership of a King, instead he corrected them by saying "The Lord shall rule over you." "The Lord" means something or someone to have authority over you. Gideon was teaching them that God has the authority over the Israelites. The same God that was with Moses and Joshua was with Gideon. God was with him because Gideon placed Him as Lord over his life and Israel. To have success in warfare and the battles that come up against you in life, you must have God as Lord over your life.

    The Israelites at times mirror the condition of some people within the Body of Christ. People within the Body of Christ have made men and material things Lord over their lives. This is the reason why they are struggling in warfare, battles, and constantly backsliding. They say with their lips "Jesus is savior and their Lord," but their hearts are far away from God. Because of this whoring that is happening with the church, these people are given over to their gods, politics, famous celebrities, money, materials, witchcraft, dark magic, and Satan himself. This is causing eyes to be blind and hearts to be hardened. The worst thing to do is wait to see how far you can go without God, and how bad it can get. Look at the history of the Israelites, they were given over to other gods and in the hands of their enemies. Due to people's own pride and stubbornness, they are upset with their circumstances, and they are angry with God that their circumstances haven't changed. Jesus can only rescue them when they finally come to terms with there being only one name that saves, Jesus. Sometimes it takes being backed up in a corner and being on the verge of death to wake up and allow God to be Lord over your life.

  The first step to victory is repentance. To repent means that you have a deep remorse for the wrong you've been doing, and you are going to do whatever it takes to change. There are different types of warfare and battles we endure. A lot of times people do not realize that they are the reason for their warfare because they refuse to accept the wrong on their part and change. Pride is blinding the eyes of those who are fully submitted to God and are not being willing and obedient. There is freedom today, have Jesus Christ be the authority over your life. The authority that casts out demons, heals the sick, tells the storms to be still, and brings us victory in Jesus. Only His name is above all names, and only He is the way, the truth, and the life. He is the only key that gives us access to God and to heaven. Those who have authority in warfare, over their appointed territories, and in their life have the Holy Spirit residing in them. The Lord over their life is Jesus. Onward mighty warrior.

Marching Orders

Judges 4:6-7, "She sent for Barak son of Abinoam from Kedesh in Naphtali and said to him, "The Lord, the God of Israel, commands you: 'Go, take with you ten thousand men of Naphtali and Zebulun and lead them up to Mount Tabor. I will lead Sisera, the commander of Jabin's army, with his chariots and his troops to the Kishon River and give him into your hands.'"

Deborah, the prophetess, was leading Israel while Israel was in the hands of Jabin the King of Canaan. The Israelites were given over to this king because they did evil in the eyes of the Lord after the death of Ehud. For twenty years they were oppressed, and they cried out to the Lord for help. God heard their cries and used Deborah to give battle orders. She sent for Barak to go to Sisera, the commander of Jabin's army and his chariots and troops and have them given over unto his hands. She gave instructions for him to take ten thousand men of Naphtali and Zebulun. Barak didn't want to go without Deborah, so she told him that the Lord will deliver Sisera into the hands of a woman. A good leader would empower others to lead and if the person is not ready to lead alone, they will go along with them and be their support.

God gives us orders, just as the military officials give military personnel orders to go into war. When we became engrafted into God's covenant, we became a part of a royal priesthood, and we received redemption, salvation, and deliverance. There is work that needs to be done here on earth before Jesus returns. Before Jesus ascended into heaven after his resurrection, He told the disciples that He will leave them a helper. He also explained to them that they will do greater works than He had done when he walked on earth. He commissioned them to go out to the world, make disciples, and to baptize people in the name of the Father, the Son, and the Holy Spirit. Jesus knew the disciples needed the Holy Spirit, the helper to support them. A good leader will support, but still push someone else to go out and do the task they are called to do and enter the battle they are assigned too.

We are assigned orders to take territory whether it be in the ministry or the marketplace. There are also assignments to obtain wealth and break generational curses. Deborah told Barak to go into battle. She stated in Judges 4:14, "Go!, This is the day the Lord has given Sisera into your hands. Has not the Lord gone ahead of you?" Then the Lord routed Sisera and all his chariots and army by the sword. Everything the Lord has for you, your victory, deliverance, financial freedom, needs for your ministry and business, the Lord has gone ahead of you. All you need to do is take action. The Lord has put that very thing in your heart, he has shown you in your prophetic imagination, and you have spoken into those areas with great faith. The last step you need to do is move.

Matthew 11:12 states, "And from the days of John the Baptist until now, the Kingdom of Heaven suffers violence, and the violent take it by force." Satan is not just going to hand over what belongs to you. The boldness and courage that is inside of you is already there. We are carriers of God's glory, and His Holy Spirit abides in us and is our helper. The Lord has gone ahead of us, and we have what we need. The lie the devil puts in a lot of people's minds is that they do not have what it takes to take every blessing that rightfully belongs to them. As a prayer warrior called to the nations, I am here to remind you that you have what it takes to take the land, the territory, the success, the financial freedom, and to start the ministry. You are more than a conqueror. We are not just here to be mere men and women hoping we will get picked like a lottery. No, we get up, pray, fight, and take what belongs to us. Deborah was a woman, a prophetess, and a judge over Israel. God doesn't determine our position or success based on our gender, race, skin color, financial or educational status. As long as there is a willing vessel and a "yes" to God to do great exploits and His Kingdom work, that is all God needs. Go and take it all, you are anointed for this.

Fearless Warrior

Judges 4:23, "On that day God subdued Jabin king of Canaan before the Israelites."

A woman named Jael, Heber's wife, met Sisera, the commander of the Canaanite army, and they went into her tent. She gave him milk after he asked for water after fleeing from Barak and his men while his army and chariots all fell by the sword. She waited for him to sleep, and she took a tent peg and a hammer and put the peg through Sisera's temple. On this day, God subdued Jabin, king of Canaan, and the Israelites became stronger and destroyed Jabin. It takes courage to stand up against Satan and forcefully take the victory over your life that rightfully belongs to you.

Jael operated with wisdom and intellect. She knew Sisera was running away from the Israelites and that he was greatly exhausted. This was a perfect opportunity to take out the enemy. In the midst of trial and spiritual warfare, what kind of thinking are you operating with? Is it true, honorable, right, pure, lovely, and admirable according to Philippians 4:8? Or is it vain imaginations, wrong, perverse, hateful, and just plain wicked?

Your thoughts are the result of the condition of your mind. This is how you determine if you have a healthy mind or sick mind. In order to succeed against the devil, your adversary, you must remain vigilant; operate in wisdom. The devil is constantly seeking ways to kill, steal, and/or destroy you and your life by keeping track of your weaknesses and strengths. This is how the enemy takes full advantage of throwing fiery darts against you with thoughts or influencing people to irritate you. The very fact that Satan knows how to attack you in your thoughts, shows that he is strategic and knows you. This should be enough fuel to fight back and subdue your enemy.

    Jael took advantage of Sisera to take him out, she was wise and did what needed to be done so that Israel could get the victory. Take advantage of the enemy by staying five steps ahead. Subdue the devil by living a holy and righteous life. Holy and righteous living leads to obedience towards God, thinking of good things, resisting temptation, and being intentional in the way you speak and handle yourself. This is enough to subdue the enemy when he throws dart after dart, arrow after arrow, attack after attack, distraction after distraction. This is bringing fatigue and weariness to Satan; it frustrates him but then it scares him. You just prove that God is Lord over your life, and you stand on His word and promises, not Satan and his lies. This drives a tent peg through the devil's temple.

Do not get caught up in battles and warfare by fighting on the defense all the time. The devil knows that you are distracted, and he keeps throwing attack after attack because it's wearing you out. This is the reason a lot of people begin to feel spiritually and mentally drained and fatigued. This is a result of constantly fighting on the defense because you are too focused on attack instead of looking for the root of the attack. Are you distracted? Is your focus off of God and the assignment he has given you? Do you have an open door that's giving Satan legal access to your life; unrepented sin, bitterness, or unforgiveness? What is the condition of your mind, are your thoughts positive or negative? What life are you pursuing, holy living or after your own fleshly desires? This is a self-evaluation that needs to be done, especially if the enemy is throwing attack after attack. The devil wants you so caught up on the attack that you're distracted from self-evaluating yourself because he wants to prevent you from bettering yourself and subduing him.

Go and get the victory. You have already won. Jesus won your victory already, know that victory is your battle stance. Equip yourself with the Word of God, train your mind to be healthy, walk-in obedience and truth, pursue God and focus on the Kingdom of God. Doing these very things, everything you desire will be added unto you. Subdue Satan and his kingdom, they already lost so get the victory in all the battles as you complete the Kingdom mandate on your life.

The Power of Worship and Praise

Judges 5:11, "They recite the victories of the Lord, the victories of his villagers in Israel."

The Song of Deborah in Judges 5 summarizes the battle of Israel with Canaan. Deborah arose as a mother of Israel. She rose up in a time of great trouble to lead the Israelites as a judge and a prophetess. She arose to be a mouthpiece for God to the Israelites, in a time when they turned to other gods, to bring an instruction that will give victory over the Canaanites. As a woman, she did not back down because of her gender and how difficult the times were. She arose, she commanded Barak with the leading of God, went to battle and overthrew Sisera and their chariots. Jael, the wife of Heber, saw Sisera retreating from the battle, and she was not afraid of him or his position. She rose up in faith and with a victorious mindset, gave him milk to put him to sleep, and she drove a tent peg through the temple of his head to take him out. Mighty women began rising up so that their people and their children could rise up and take back what belonged to them. This mighty and bold move is enough to praise the Lord, showing that anyone is capable of rising up to take the victory for the Kingdom of God.

Warriors sing praises unto the Lord in battle. We praise God in the midst of the battles, and we praise God when we win the battle. The sound of praise shakes the heavens and breaks barriers the enemy has set up before you. Praise takes back the very blessings and provision the enemy has stolen from you. The song of praise brings great misery to the enemy. Your praise is a weapon, it is very vital and important to use in your prayers, and daily walk. The praise of victory defeats Satan and weakens his army. We go into battle knowing we have the victory. Christ gave us the victory on the cross and He rose again; so, we are no longer bound by a life of sin and struggle. The limitation was broken off and we were given full access to God through Jesus Christ.

To grab the concept that we have unlimited access to our Father should stir up great confidence and courage in us. We enter the gates with praise and thanksgiving, then we surrender and let go of every burden that weighs us down, and finally our praises ushers us into the Holy of Holies. How beautiful and wonderful this is singing with the angels, singing our praises, and worshiping God. We have unlimited access to our God; He is an infinite being. The assignment we are called to, the Lord has already gone before us, all He needs us to do is go forth praising Him.

Praising and singing songs of worship and victory builds up courage and self-confidence. We are filled with a spirit of boldness, and we receive the revelation that all things are possible through Christ Jesus. We sing old hymns and hymns of the Bible, and it reminds us of our victories, breakthroughs, and how much the Lord is with us. The thought of not being able to achieve success in a spiritual battle with overcoming the lust of your flesh, financial breakthrough, and/or building a ministry soon withers away because we know the God we serve. God wants us to rise up for such a time as this. Your gender, age, and experience does not determine if you are qualified. The Lord anoints you to do the work of his Kingdom. He has already anointed you and equipped you. Now He is calling you to rise up. Rise up prayer warrior. Now is your time to arise and shine. Take the territory, pray until strongholds are broken, and drive the enemy out the land. God has lifted a standard.

www.ingramcontent.com/pod-product-compliance
Lightning Source LLC
Chambersburg PA
CBHW070323100426
42743CB00011B/2534